KINGFISHERS

First published in Great Britain in 1997 by
Colin Baxter Photography Ltd.,
Grantown-on-Spey,
Moray PH26 3NA
Scotland

A CIP Catalogue record for this book is available from the British Library

ISBN 1-900455-25-0

Printed in Hong Kong

KINGFISHERS

Charlie Hamilton James

Colin Baxter Photography, Grantown-on-Spey, Scotland

Contents

Kingfishers

For those lucky enough to see a kingfisher it usually appears as a brilliant flash of blue, which disappears as quickly as it came; only the memory seems to last forever. It is, however, not only the kingfishers' stunning plumage that makes them such special birds; it is also their behaviour, adaptations and individuality. They have given rise to myth and legend as far back as the ancient Greeks with special powers being attributed to this 'halcyon bird', such as the ability to ward off evil spirits, bring good luck and calm the sea.

When most people see a kingfisher for the first time, they are amazed by how small it is, being not much larger than a robin, around $6\frac{1}{2}$ in (17 cm) from tip to tail and weighing just over 1 oz (36–37g). Kingfishers have petite bodies, with slightly oversized heads and long dagger-like bills. The tail is short and stumpy, as are the wings, which means that they have to beat their wings rapidly to keep themselves in the air. Sexes are similar, the only external difference being that the male has a black beak and the female has an orange streak along her lower mandible. The feet are a deep pink/red colour in the adults and black in the juveniles – a feature which not only provides kingfisher watchers but also the birds themselves with a guide to the maturity of an individual.

The kingfisher's colours are its hallmark. The function of the colouration is supposed to be to make a statement to would-be predators that they are distasteful and should not be eaten. This does not always work, however, because kingfishers are taken by rats, weasels, mink and especially sparrowhawks. Despite its very bright colours, a motionless kingfisher can remain fairly well camouflaged amongst the undergrowth along the river. Their bright feather colours are not due to true pigment, for pure blue pigment does not actually exist in birds. Rather, the astonishing colours on the upper parts of the kingfisher are the result of a complex structure in the layers of the feathers which filters out certain colours of light, reflecting back only blue. This is known as the 'Tyndal effect' and as a result of it the kingfisher can appear to turn from bright blue to a rich emerald green with only a slight change in the angle at which the light falls on it.

The blue covers the top of the head, the wings, the back and the tail with a little streak across the face. The most spectacular of the blues streaks down the back from the neck to the tail and is such a rich colour that it is almost impossible to recreate through painting or photography. The breast is a chestnut orange, as is the underside of the tail and wings, which may make the bird appear like a falling leaf to fish as the kingfisher dives. The throat and ear coverts are white. Around each eye are two orange patches which occasionally link. The one in front of the eye is small and the larger stretches under the eye into the ear coverts. The eye itself is black and brown; around it are tiny lashes which, if you are a photographer, are excellent for focusing on.

A fleeting flash of blue along the riverbank is often the closest a casual observer will get to seeing the kingfisher in action.

Some books report that the plumage of the female is not as brilliant as that of the male, but I have only found this to be so with one female and would not agree that it is the case with all female kingfishers. In some pairs that I have observed, the female is slightly larger and plumper than the male. Kingfishers, however, are able to make themselves appear slimmer or plumper by drawing in or puffing up their feathers.

Adult male kingfishers perform threatening manoeuvres to ward off unwanted competition from their territory.

The Kingfisher Family

The kingfisher family is actually rather large and diverse. The 90 or so species across the world vary in colour, size, habit and distribution – from the kookaburra of Australia to the strange shovel-billed kingfisher of Papua New Guinea. It is not possible to be precise about how many different species there are as accounts vary, but it is probably between 85 and 95. Several of them are endangered, and some are known only from rare sightings or the discovery of their skins. All are members of an order of birds known as the Coraciiformes, comprising seven families – kingfishers, rollers, hoopoes, bee-eaters, hornbills, motmots and todies. Although these birds do not all look alike they are linked in the evolutionary tree and share a number of characteristics – all have 'syndactyl feet'(their third and fourth toe digits are fused for half of their length); none build nests, preferring to excavate burrows in banks or find holes in trees; and all are predominantly carnivorous or piscivorous.

The kingfisher family is known as the Alcedinidae, and split into three main sub-families – Alcedininae, Daceloninae and Cerylinae. The Alcedininae are the 'fishing' kingfishers. There are 22 species in this sub-family, including *Alcedo atthis* found throughout the world. They are the most colourful of the kingfishers, with a stunning bright plumage – the paradise kingfishers being supreme examples. The alcedinids are small and squat, with narrow, slender bills. They live almost exclusively near water, feeding mainly on fish and other aquatic animals, and nesting in river banks.

The Daceloninae are the forest kingfishers, such as the kookaburra. They are not dependent on water for their survival, living mainly in forests and scrubland and feeding on snakes, lizards, insects and small vertebrates. Unlike the more flighty, active Alcedininae, the dacelonids are more prepared to sit and wait for their prey. They are generally larger than the Alcedininae and nest in termite mounds and tree holes. There are 55 kingfisher species in this sub-family.

The Cerylinae is made up of nine species ranging from south-east Asia through Africa to America. All are riverine and have similar habits to the Alcedininae. Most noteworthy in this sub-family is the pied kingfisher *Ceryl rudis*, for it is one of the few kingfishers that is not predominantly solitary, often seen in small groups and nesting in colonies. The pied kingfisher is an expert hoverer and is the only kingfisher able to catch and eat its prey without returning to a perch, enabling it to hunt out at sea and on the great lakes of Africa. The cerylids lack the stunning colours of the alcedinids, yet the patterns of the pied kingfisher make it an exceptionally beautiful bird.

The most widespread of all kingfishers is the species which lives in Britain – *Alcedo atthis*. Its range extends from Europe across Asia to the Orient and down to the Pacific Islands. It is found in few areas of northern and east Africa and throughout mid and southern Russia. There are nine sub-species of *Alcedo atthis*, which vary in size and colour, and according to geography. The British form, *A. a. ispida*, ranges across northern and western Europe, south to Portugal and Iraq. The nominate form *A. a. atthis* is found beyond this range and extends from the Mediterranean to south-west Asia. It is a little smaller than *ispida* and has a more slender bill and slightly duller plumage. Other forms include *A. a. bengalensis*, *A. a. taprobana*, *A. a. pallasii*, *A. a. hispidoides*, *A. a. floresiana*, *A. a. solomonensis* and *A. a. japonica*.

There are two other species of kingfishers in Europe, these are the White-breasted kingfisher, *Halcyon smyrensis*, and the pied kingfisher *Ceryle rudis*, both are restricted to southern Europe. This book concentrates on the British species, the Eurasian kingfisher *Alcedo atthis*.

Distribution

The Eurasian kingfisher is seldom seen due to its elusive behaviour and shyness. It ranges across almost the entire country, although it is absent from the north of Scotland in the winter months. Kingfishers are present in Ireland but, strangely, absent from the north-west tip.

In the UK, their habitats vary widely. Rivers and streams predominate although kingfishers are also found on lakes, canals and estuaries. Large lakes which form in peat cuttings and gravel pools are perfect places for sticklebacks, and kingfishers will

An intricate pattern of feathers makes up the distinctive markings of the adult kingfisher.

also breed and live around such lakes, feeding almost entirely on the stickleback. Kingfishers are also prepared to make their home in urban areas. I have seen them in city centres, including Bristol and Oxford. One memorable sighting was at Bath Spa station, where the bird flew right through the station between the railway tracks!

Kingfishers are territorial and protect their patch fiercely. Their territories vary in size, usually being 2–3 miles (3–5 km) long on a river with adequate fish stocks, though they can be larger if fish populations are small. They can also be much smaller, in some cases territories do not exist at all and several kingfishers will live alongside each other. This is certainly true of some of the large rivers in the south-west of France, where I have seen upwards of ten individuals together.

Clean rivers are essential for kingfisher populations and a fairly large supply of small fish is needed, especially during the summer months, to enable the birds to breed successfully. Britain fares well within Europe, with 4000–6000 pairs of kingfishers. Italy and France have similar populations, and Ireland has a population of 1300–2100 pairs. These high numbers are a direct result of well kept waterways. However, these figures are only relative; the population of kingfishers in the UK fluctuates but is slowly declining. Kingfishers are extremely sensitive to river pollution. In countries with more river pollution kingfishers suffer badly; in Luxembourg for instance, there are thought to be only 65–90 pairs and these are found in the north of the country where the rivers are cleaner. Further south they have all but disappeared.

Cold winters significantly affect kingfisher populations; numbers can drop dramatically within a very short period of time, as rivers and lakes freeze over and cap their food supply. In Germany, kingfishers are known as 'the ice birds' as they migrate south at the first sign of frost, returning in the spring. British kingfishers seldom leave the country, yet they do travel around, coming south in winter, but they rarely cross the channel. Kingfishers will sometimes go to the coast in winter however, where they feed on shrimps and other marine life. Kingfishers in continental Europe tend to be more migratory than those in Great Britain; this may be related to the high population density in the UK.

Lifestyle

Territory

The kingfisher's territory is basically its home range. However, this is so fiercely guarded that it is referred to as a territory. A good territory must contain a number of important characteristics. It must have: a plentiful supply of small fish; cover provided by trees and undergrowth; a high vertical bank suitable for nesting; and a number of areas of still water. As such territories are hard to find in the UK, kingfishers will protect their stretch of river or lake aggressively, displaying to any intruders and attacking them if necessary. The territory is occupied for most of the year by a single bird, although it is fairly common for two individuals of the opposite sex to overlap their territories and they will most likely become partners during the breeding season. In cases like this, however, there always remains an air of tension, especially over good fishing spots.

Territorial disputes are most common in the summer months, when there is a surge in the population as the fledgling kingfishers are expelled by their parents from the territory and go off to find a stretch of river of their own. Often they will simply fly down river to the next territory and hang around there until they are discovered by the parent birds and driven away.

Kingfishers have a fairly defined way of dealing with intruders. If the intruder is a young bird it is not taken very seriously and often just flown at and harassed. If, however, the intruder is older it is treated with more caution. The first reaction of an occupying bird upon seeing an intruder is to fly at it and chase it, whistling loudly and continuously – a high-pitched 'swissoo' sound. If this does not work both birds will stop on perches only a few feet apart and start displaying and whistling. When this happens the birds almost go into a trance, adopting specific postures and movements. Immediately upon landing the tail will splay and the beak will be open. The feathers are drawn tight against the body, the wings drop and the bill is poked forward. The birds then move their heads slowly from side to side. From this pose they will drop their heads down and hunch up their rumps. This sequence will occur repeatedly for as long as the dispute lasts and whistling will continue sporadically throughout the display. Most disagreements are resolved fairly speedily, within an hour; sometimes, however, they can go on much longer, with both birds holding their ground.

In extreme cases, when disputes cannot be resolved amicably, fights can result in death by drowning. The birds will lock beaks and attempt to push each other into the water, sometimes both falling in and continuing the fight afloat. But this is very rare and in the 11 years that I have been watching kingfishers, I have only once seen two males trying to drown each other.

Breeding and courtship

Not all kingfishers pair for life, although some do; more commonly the male and female with adjoining territories will breed together, splitting the territories at the end of the season. If this does not happen, birds with the urge to reproduce will travel to find a mate and a new territory. This, of course, causes a lot of confusion and hard work for birds trying to defend their patches.

The first signs of the breeding season usually start between the middle and end of February, although this can be later in the north of the country. When the pair first meet they become very excited, calling to each other and chasing each other up and down the river. They stop occasionally and call to each other, the male making most of the noise, whistling a 'swissoo' every couple of minutes, which is replied to with a similar sound. At this point it is quite common for the male bird to sit high up in a tree and whistle to the female below; indeed, some of the flight chases can be performed high in the air, above the tops of the trees. When one of the birds takes off down the river the other will follow and the calls rise to a crescendo of single high-pitched whistles. These are very loud and similar to those used when territorial disputes are taking place; in fact there remains a degree of tension, such as this whistling, throughout the early stages of the courtship process.

A lot of the tension subsides when the male makes the step of catching the

*Hidden amongst the thick vegetation of the riverbank, the kingfisher's burrow
proves a challenge for all but the most persistent predators.*

first 'engagement' fish for the female and feeding it to her. She may make this difficult for him at first and seems 'to play hard to get'; however, once she accepts it the bond is formed and the two birds become a pair. The feeding of fish by the male to the female lasts until the two birds have successfully mated.

The next step of the breeding process is nest building; it is important that the pair live in a territory with a number of high mud banks as this is where the birds nest. A perfect nest bank is next to water, between 5 and 10 ft (1.5 and 3 m) high with a thick cover on the top. The soil must not be too hard or full of stones. The bank must be vertical – kingfishers will never nest in a bank that slopes down to the water as this would render them even more vulnerable to predators. Occasionally when suitable nest banks cannot be found kingfishers have been known to nest in holes in trees and walls, sometimes hundreds of yards from water.

Once the pair has established a suitable bank the digging begins. The male will do the initial groundwork, flying at the bank and stabbing it with his bill, eventually forming a small indentation which he can get a grip on. From this he can start to tunnel inwards. Both birds then play their part in the excavation, sitting next to each other on a convenient perch and taking their turns with the digging.

The tunnel is usually closer to the top of the bank than the bottom and inclines slightly downwards towards the entrance; this helps to drain debris from the nest area and protect it against flooding and predation; rivers in spate can rise very rapidly and low nests are often flooded. One nest that I found was only 18 in (45 cm) above the river, in the root system below a tree, it was very inaccessible to predators but one heavy rainstorm would have flooded it within hours.

The nest digging, depending on the compaction of the soil, can last for up to two weeks, although in good earth it can be much quicker. If a stone is encountered half way in, the tunnel will often be abandoned and another one started; sometimes several semi-made holes are found right next to each other. When complete the tunnel is usually about 2 ft (60 cm) in length, although sometimes as little as 9 in (22 cm), with a well rounded chamber at the end.

After the nest is complete, usually around the beginning of April, the kingfishers mate. This happens several times over a few days to ensure fertilisation. I have only witnessed this spectacle twice and to my regret I have never managed to photograph it. The first time I saw it I was standing on a bridge watching a female bird preening. From down river I heard the whistle of the male as he flew up river, under the bridge, to a branch not far from the female. He whistled again and flew onto the branch next to her. They exchanged whistles and he flew up, hovered above her and landed on her back, gripping the feathers on her nape with his beak and flapping his wings in order to keep balance. This lasted for only a few seconds before he flew off down stream, whistling. The whole process, from his arrival, had lasted less than a minute.

The second time I witnessed kingfishers mating I was in my hide. Both birds flew up and sat next to each other, for a few minutes, only 6 ft (1.8 m) away from me whistling occasionally and then mated. The male bird will often present the female with a fish before copulation; if she refuses it he will not be allowed to mount her and she will become aggressive if he tries.

Mating will continue until the completion of the clutch in the nest. The eggs, which are almost round, are laid separately, one a day, for a week – seven eggs in a clutch being average. In common with all tunnel-nesting birds, the pure white eggs are laid well out of sight of prying eyes, so there is no need for them to be camouflaged. This may also help the adult bird see them in the darkness of the tunnel so it can turn and attend them. They are usually laid in the early part of the morning, often at the same time every day, onto the bare soil of the nest chamber.

The female will do most of the incubation for the first few days, but she does not begin until all the eggs have been laid; this is fairly common among birds and it ensures that all the eggs hatch at roughly the same time.

After a couple of days the male bird starts to take on more of the incubation, sharing the work load, allowing the female to feed and preen. Each incubation session lasts usually for 1–2 hours. The sitting bird will wait until it hears its mate

whistling down the river; it will then leave the nest to let its mate fly in. Once out of the nest the kingfisher will fly to a favourite perch and feed and preen, diving into the water to clean the dirt from its feathers.

Incubation lasts from 18–21 days and the chicks are born blind, naked and ugly. They huddle their little pink bodies together in the nest to keep warm and look as if they are constantly shivering. At this point they are extremely vulnerable, probably more so than at any other stage in the nesting. If the parents leave the nest and are not able to return due to disturbance, the chicks will die. It only takes a fisherman or a family picnicking near the nest for as little as an hour; in this time the body temperature of the chicks can drop to a point where they can not reheat and they die of hypothermia within a few hours. I have seen this happen once, in Somerset. The kingfishers were nesting in a bank next to a usually quiet road. It was a particularly cold spring and the chicks were already suffering from having an inexperienced father who failed to feed them very often. At about eight o'clock in the evening the female left the nest to fish; before she could fly back to the nest, cars started to drive up the road in unusually high numbers. This went on for an hour; people were getting out of their cars and wandering around in the river. Attempts to remove them failed, they were on a village treasure hunt and were stopping for no-one.

Eventually after an hour and a half the female managed to return to the nest where she stayed until the morning. Assuming everything to be fine, the filming that we were doing went on as normal; however the behaviour of the parent birds became so strange that we eventually inspected the nest to find all seven chicks dead. I watched the nest for several days after that and saw the birds revisit it, but I never found out whether they re-nested in it. I did, however, find a wren's nest just upstream made out of kingfisher feathers. I can only assume these were from an adult male, and that a younger, inexperienced male bird had taken over the dead bird's territory with the female. Incidents like this must happen all the time across the country. Unless you are familiar with kingfishers, you could not be aware of any disturbance being caused to them.

For the first few days after hatching the chicks are fed very small fish, sometimes only about ¼ in (1 cm) long. The parent birds take turns fishing, returning to the nest fairly regularly throughout the day, usually being more active in the early morning and evening with a little spree at lunchtime. The bird that is not fishing will tend to the chicks and keep them warm, puffing up its breast feathers and sitting on top of them. When the fishing bird returns to the nest with the fish, it flies in, blocking out the only light source entering the nest; the chicks respond to this and chirp weakly; they shuffle into position, opening their beaks and raising their heads. The adult bird moves up the tunnel and gently feeds the fish, headfirst, to the closest chick. The chicks take their turn at the front of the nest chamber, rotating round to ensure that they all get fed. When fish stocks are low, smaller chicks will often lose out to larger, stronger ones which require more food. This is common among birds and usually results in the slow starvation of the smaller chicks.

After a few days, areas of what looks like bruising appear on the chicks; these are the beginnings of quills, which ultimately turn into feathers. Each day the areas of blue become larger and darker, and eventually the quills break through the skin. After eight or nine days, the large bulging eyes begin to open, allowing the chicks for the first time to see their parents entering the nest hole. By this time the parents have almost stopped brooding them and are bringing larger fish back to the apparently eternally ravenous chicks. By the time the chicks are 15 or 16 days old they are beginning to look more like kingfishers. Quills cover their bodies almost completely, although they have not broken, and their beaks are full size. They become very loud when they hear a parent bird whistling down stream and wrestle with each other over the fish.

This last week before fledging is a very busy period for the parent birds which are having to bring fish back to the nest almost continuously. I once spent a morning photographing a nest at this stage and ran off two rolls of film within an hour. The parents were feeding the chicks on average every two minutes. This could not have lasted continuously throughout the day but I stayed for two hours and they were

*Providing enough food for young chicks growing in their burrow
is a constant job for both parents.*

The closest chick to the burrow opening receives the fish from its parent, before being replaced by a hungry sibling ready for the next visit.

still going strong when I left.

This period is often when the parent birds will start thinking about a second brood. It is common for kingfishers to have two broods in one year. The pair on the river I watch over usually managed three broods, and in one year they managed four; not only that but they had all four in the same nest hole! This is extremely rare behaviour, however, and the two broods that they average are more usually in separate nest holes. This ability to raise so many chicks in one year can enable king-fisher populations to rise much faster following severe winters. If there is a good supply of fish in the river the male has time to start excavating a new nest within a few days of the first brood hatching. The demands on him are not too high for the first few days of the hatching so he will spend his spare time digging. The female bird can then start laying her new clutch before the first brood of chicks has fledged.

Fledging

Fledging takes place after 23–24 days, by this time the chicks look like large dull versions of their parents. They usually leave the nest in the early morning, having been building up their courage for some time, with trips down to the end of the tunnel and back. The parent birds will whistle outside the nest and reduce the amount of feeding to try and encourage them out. Eventually one will build up the courage to leave, which undoubtedly encourages the others, and it makes its first dangerous flight across the river to the nearest branch. This is the second most dangerous time for the young kingfishers when they can easily die from drowning or depredation. Once they have all left the nest they will fly up and down river, often accompanied by a parent, until they find an area which they like, and where they will settle. They will all congregate on this stretch of river, sometimes sitting only a few feet apart, and learn 'the ropes'.

The fledglings remain fairly well hidden for the first few days, sitting in amongst the vegetation along the edge of the river. They are not the beautiful striking blue of their parents at this age and are remarkably well camouflaged. It takes several months to look like an adult kingfisher, the birds must go through their first moult and their stumpy beaks and tails must become longer and more slender. The most noticeable physical difference between a juvenile and an adult is the white tip on the end of the juvenile's otherwise black beak. This remains for several weeks. Juvenile kingfishers also have black feet, rather than the bright red ones their parents sport. These begin to change colour after fledging and the undersides will begin to turn pink within two weeks, becoming redder as the bird matures. Immediately after fledging the young birds have a mottled blue/grey crown around their chest which fades within the first two weeks. Sexes are not easily distinguishable just after fledging, the females lacking the red strip on the lower mandible. This varies in the time it takes to appear. In some broods females obtain their first signs of redness within a week, but it can often take a few months. The young birds lack the obvious agility of their parents and bob up and down continuously. They also have an amazing ability to sit and do absolutely nothing for hours, which if you are trying to photograph them isn't much fun, especially as they can do this on the roof of the hide!

The parents continue to bring fish to the fledglings, feeding them on which ever branch they have taken up residence, or, if they can't find them, flying up river whistling until they are whistled back at or followed. The young do try to catch fish for themselves but rarely succeed and will quite often return to their perch with a stone or a leaf; it is very amusing to watch a juvenile kingfisher try to kill and eat a willow leaf.

The chicks have a lot to learn at this age; they often make too many unsuccessful dives without preening in between and become waterlogged, running the risk of drowning. Once they become more adept at fishing they have to learn what they can and cannot eat. Sticklebacks, for instance, can be a danger, having very sharp spines along their backs and flanks. Adult kingfishers treat them with caution and make sure that they are totally dead before eating them, as once dead the spines flatten. One young kingfisher once caught a stickleback in front of my hide and after a very superficial attempt to kill it proceeded to try and swallow it. When

Taking a break from feeding their brood, a male and female
kingfisher pause on a nearby branch.

In order to survive and avoid territorial disputes, adolescent
kingfishers often attach themselves to a nearby fledging brood, often going
unnoticed for some time by the adult birds.

the fish was half swallowed and still thrashing it became stuck. For 15 minutes the young bird tried to regurgitate the fish, shaking its head and wrenching at the fish, but it was stuck. By the time the bird managed to swallow the fish it had begun to shiver and sway on the perch. It had come very close to death and it was probably only the fact that the stickleback had suffocated whilst in its throat that saved it. I watched the same bird catch a stickleback the next day, it spent two or three minutes smashing the fish's head against the perch, killing it several times over, before swallowing it!

Within a few days of leaving the nest the affection of the parent birds begins to wane. They no longer feed their chicks, and they harass them when they see them. This becomes progressively worse until, after a week and a half, they no longer want anything to do with the fledglings, flying at them and chasing them whenever they are spotted along the river. This is yet another hard time for the chicks as they have the choice of leaving to find their own territory or staying and putting up with the harassment and aggression for a little longer. Most of them will leave within the first two weeks and try to fend for themselves, finding new territories or poaching in others. Finding a new territory can be difficult for young kingfishers. There is a surge in the population throughout the summer, and all the young birds leave their parent territory and try to find their own. Young birds may often be forced to take less desirable territories, or be continually chased off by birds already resident. Mortality at this stage in the kingfisher's life is high – as much as 80% – and many die before they have found a territory. They are killed by predators, starvation, drowning, or by collision with cars and windows. I was given the body of one young kingfisher two weeks before the completion of this book. She had caused quite a stir when she flew into the window of the BBC Bristol canteen, killing herself instantly. I estimated that she was only six weeks old. The surprising thing about her death was not that she had flown into the window, but that she had flown into the window in central Bristol.

Some of the fledglings will decide to stay on and poach from their parents' territory. They become very elusive and alert, often sitting in the vegetation at the side of the river, remaining almost totally silent and vanishing the moment they hear a parent bird whistling down the river. The parent birds react aggressively towards the fledgings if they catch them. Adults are highly territorial at this stage; they are being invaded continually by their own offspring and by other rogue juveniles in the area.

Occasionally youngsters born early in the season will leave their territories and take up residence in a territory where the young of the resident birds have just fledged. Here they can fish alongside the fledglings without being noticed by the parents. I watched one young female spend two weeks doing this; she arrived at the same time as the fledglings and fished alongside the juveniles and the mother bird without ever getting hassled. It was only the male bird that would spot the difference and attempt to drive her out. By the time all of the other youngsters had left the territory she was being positively aggressive to the resident parents.

Glass windows are often the cause of death for young birds.

What can occur in instances like this, although it is rare, is that the young bird eventually recognises the territory as its own and becomes far more reluctant to relinquish it; resulting in far more serious aggression between the territory holder and the rogue bird, which can ultimately lead to the expulsion of the resident bird. More often, however, the resident bird is older and wiser and the bond with its territory much stronger.

Feeding and Diet

Kingfishers are masters of fishing, able to spot tiny fish through reflecting water and dive at them so fast and accurately that the fish do not even have time to take evasive action – what's more they do it with their eyes shut. Kingfishers are perfectly designed for fishing, with their short legs and tails, slender bodies and long sharp bills. These make them a serious threat to any life-loving minnow. Their diet consists mainly of several species that are relatively common throughout the rivers, lakes and streams of the British Isles, such as minnows, sticklebacks, bullheads and gudgeon. Fry of larger fish such as trout and roach are eaten also, but most kingfishers usually choose bullheads. These small, ugly fish, also known as the miller's thumb, are nocturnal and live under stones in the slow-moving parts of the rivers. Minnows, certainly along the river where I observe kingfishers, were more often eaten, as they are far more plentiful and tend to shoal in large numbers throughout the day. They are often fed to newly hatched kingfishers, as they are slender and smooth, compared with the bulk of a bullhead or the sharp spines of the stickleback.

The diet of any particular bird depends entirely on what is in its territory. Kingfishers in areas of the Somerset levels will feed almost exclusively on stickleback, hunting the small man-made drainage ditches where sticklebacks congregate in large numbers. Some kingfishers live near trout hatcheries, and so trout make up a substantial part of their diet. This doesn't have to be made up exclusively of fish: I have seen adult kingfishers catch frogs and feed them to their chicks; newts and insect larvae are also taken. The kingfishers along the river I watch would often take mayflies during the big hatch in late May and early June, flying up to catch them in mid air. In harsh winters when food is scarce they will occasionally poach goldfish from ponds, creating a wonderful spectacle for the pond owner!

Not all of the fish found in the river are eaten. Stone loaches, strange catfish-like bottom feeders, are not preferred by kingfishers although they are eaten when nothing else is available.

A TV cameraman and I once tried to film kingfishers eating elvers (young eels). We wanted a shot of the bird flying into the water and catching an elver. The camera was positioned underneath a tank that the bird would dive into. The problem that we faced was the obvious one of the kingfisher's diet, and the lack of elvers within it. We tried, unsuccessfully, to get the bird to take the elvers and eventually had to use trickery. Instead of just elvers, we put a few fish into the bottom of the tank, then a layer of stretched clingfilm, then more water with elvers in. The result was that the kingfisher dived at the fish, straight through the clingfilm which broke to the edges of the tank on impact, caught a fish and returned triumphantly to its perch. The film was fine, and although it was obvious that the bird had caught a large bullhead, no-one seemed to mind.

Each bird will have its preferred food and its own way of catching it. Most will have a favourite perch, or several within their territory and most of their hunting will be done from these. They are usually a few feet above a slow-moving area of the river where there is a good supply of fish. Sticks poking out of the river bank seem to be preferred and the tell-tale white splatterings behind the perch are a good clue. Vertical stumps are not generally favoured, fence posts along the river are enjoyed, but nothing beats a good horizontal stick an inch or so thick with a lot of room to manoeuvre wings and fish. Kingfishers will often spend hours on their favourite perches, preening, fishing and gazing at the world around them, and this is especially true in winter.

There are two obvious problems that confront a kingfisher when it has chosen a fish to catch – reflection and refraction. They have managed to overcome these problems, however. Their eyes work like polarizing filters, dulling reflections from the water and giving them a view beneath the surface. They can also deal with refraction, where light is bent as it enters the water, giving objects in the water the appearance of being in a slightly different location from where they really are. Kingfishers must correct the refraction as they need to be totally accurate when

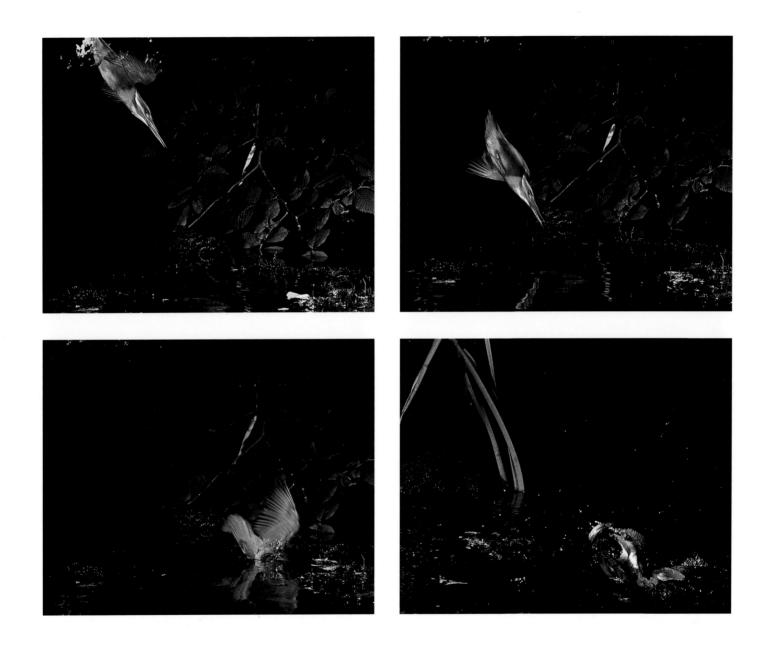

Modern photographic techniques allow the secrets of the kingfisher's lightning swoop for fish to be captured in all its intricate detail – the darting flight, breaking through the water and surfacing with a fish.

diving; this is probably learnt during the first few weeks after leaving the nest. Kingfishers' eyesight is astonishing, they can not only make the prementioned adjustments, but they can spot tiny camouflaged fish on the river bed at amazing distances, probably as much a 30 ft (9 m) even through flowing, rippled water.

A typical fishing sequence takes this form. The kingfisher flies up stream, chirping once or twice before alighting on its favoured perch. Almost immediately it looks at the water below and starts craning its neck and following the fish below it with its eyes. When it has chosen a fish it goes into a snake-like posture, feathers drawn right into the body with the neck elongated and the head well forward. While it is doing this it will be positioning itself on the perch. When it is ready it will dive, launching itself with its feet and wings off the perch towards the fish. As it nears the water its wings will draw back, making it more streamlined, its beak will open slightly and a blue membrane will sweep across its eyes to protect them.

Upon entering the water the head will lunge forward until the beak touches the fish, at which time it will shut. Kingfishers do not, as is often thought, stab the fish with their beaks but grasp it, holding it firmly between the two mandibles. The wings will already have started to push down, as if the bird were flying, which, combined with the bird's natural buoyancy, forces it to the surface. The bird then uses all its energy to break free of the water, pushing down with its

Breaking free of the water.

wings and turning into its upward flight path; at this point it knows where it intends to land, and flies back up to the perch in a shower of water droplets. This whole sequence, depending on the height of the perch, usually lasts for less than two seconds, the time spent under water being less than half a second.

Kingfishers can dive from just about any height and angle. If the flight path is obstructed or difficult it is adjusted on the way down. If the perch is within a few inches of the fish the bird will fly upwards before beginning its dive. If a photographer decides to fire his camera armed with two large flash guns as the bird dives it will hover briefly and look at the source of the disturbance. They rarely dive more than 1 ft (30 cm) under the water as deep dives are far less accurate, preferring to dive in relatively shallow water, where they attain higher success rates.

In the absence of a perch, kingfishers will hover. They can only maintain a hover for a few seconds but this is usually enough. It is quite stunning to watch, the birds often hovering 10–15 ft (3–4 m) above the water, holding their heads totally still before plunging in and re-appearing with a fish. If their perch is 10 ft (3 m) or more from the fish that they have chosen a brief hover is often used before plunging in.

Upon returning to the perch the fish will be adjusted in the beak until it is held by its tail. The kingfisher will then batter the fish's head against the perch until it is stunned or dead. A few hits on a minnow are usually enough, and they are often eaten alive and kicking! Bullheads require a little bit more violence and stickle-backs are battered until they are dead. The fish is then readjusted in the beak and swallowed head first. If the bird has young or is feeding a mate it will turn the fish around so that it can be fed to the other bird head first.

A brief flutter of feathers and a wiping of the beak on the perch follows a meal. Quite often the bird will catch two or three fish at one sitting, even four or five, depending on how hungry it is. In order to digest the fish effectively the kingfisher must produce pellets. These are made of indigestible fish bone and are usually small, light brown and oval-shaped. If the kingfisher is about to produce a pellet it will not fish, although it may look as if it is going to. Eventually it reveals why it hasn't caught anything as it opens its beak wide and starts convulsing; as the

pellet comes out the bird shakes its head and the pellet falls to the water where it separates. The bird will often catch a fish within seconds of producing a pellet.

Kingfishers are very fond of a good preen after fishing. This is essential to the health of the feathers. Preening is done very methodically and a good session lasts from 15–30 minutes, depending on how busy the bird is; it can be much longer during the autumn and winter months when the bird is not busy rearing young. In order to waterproof the feathers they must be tucked into position and re-oiled with oil from the preen gland which is found beneath the feathers. This is done with the beak over its breast and wings, moving on to use its feet to scratch the back of its head, contorting into amazing positions to do this. The bird also stretches in different ways as it preens; the wings are individually stretched, they are fully splayed out and moved around behind the bird. It will also squat down and push both wings back to stretch them. Finally at the end of the preen the kingfisher will stretch its entire body forward, lift its wings up and yawn.

Preening is vital for the kingfisher, keeping the right balance of oils on the feathers to prevent them becoming waterlogged during hunting. If this happens the bird can fail to take off from the water after a dive and will drown.

Young kingfishers fail to preen thoroughly enough, with sometimes fatal consequences. Too many failed dives, followed by short preening sessions, can leave their feathers waterlogged, which can eventually drown the bird. I have seen many come close to drowing, sometimes having to flap through the water to the river's edge after a dive.

Preening can be the best time to see the full beauty of the kingfisher's plumage as it stretches and contorts to reach every area.

Watching Kingfishers

Most healthy rivers and streams in England, Wales and southern Scotland with a good supply of fish and adequate tree cover, will have a resident kingfisher population. Once you have found such a river, and a suitable, concealed place, it is then a question of watching and waiting. Kingfishers will fly up and down their territory every few hours, checking it for intruders, which makes them fairly easy to spot. As it flies down the river it will often whistle; it is hard to describe the sound accurately – just listen out for a very loud high-pitched whistle. If you know this sound your sight rate will probably triple.

To study kingfishers at close range, you will need a hide. My first was an old Land Rover tarpaulin draped over my head next to the kingfisher's favourite perch. The bird appeared within minutes of me hiding under the canvas and sat 3 ft (1m) away. This was a lucky first attempt. Keep the hide at least 20 ft (6 m) away at first, maybe moving closer as the kingfisher becomes more accepting.

The really serious watcher and photographer will need to use a fish pool, made of anything that will stop fish escaping. I use an old white enamel bowl which the kingfishers have become used to, allowing me to move it throughout the territory and get results fast. You will need to catch fish for the pool (the hardest part of all) which should then be positioned in the flight path of the kingfisher. If there are no suitable perches next to the pool, erect one for them; it should be horizontal, allowing the birds some room for manoeuvre.

Kingfisher nests should be avoided by anyone but experts. It is an offence to watch or photograph kingfishers in or near the nest as they are protected under the Wildlife and Countryside Act 1981. Licences to research the birds can be obtained in Britain from English Nature, the Countryside Council for Wales or Scottish Natural Heritage.

I have spent 11 years trying to perfect the art of watching and photographing kingfishers and I am still learning. All I can say is read the books and be patient; there is a lot to learn. When you get your first close-up sighting and see a spectacle that nature keeps so well hidden, your patience seems well rewarded.

KINGFISHER FACTS

European Kingfisher

Latin Name:	*Alcedo atthis*
Length:	6 ½ in (17 cm) from tip to tail
Weight:	1 oz (36–27 g)
Breeding season:	March to August
Clutch size:	5–7 eggs
Incubation period:	18–21 days
Fledging period:	23–24 days
Mortality of young:	2–3 nestlings survive from a clutch of 7 eggs
Population in UK:	4000–6000 pairs
Distribution in UK:	Across UK; rare in Scotland, and absent from northern Scotland in winter. Also present in Northern Ireland except north-west tip.

Sub-species of Alcedo Atthis

*A. a. atthis, A. a. ispida, A. a. bengalenis, A. a. taprobana, A. a. pallasii,
A. a. hispidoides, A. a. floresiana, A. a. solomonensis*

Recommended Reading

The book which most influenced me as a child was *The Kingfisher* by David Boag, published by Blandford Press (1982). The text is extremely comprehensive, giving all the information you need to appreciate kingfishers. This book is difficult to get hold of now but can still be found in libraries.

Another excellent book is *Kingfisher* by Paolo Fioratti, published by Harper Collins. The text is concise and the photographs are stunning.

Also refer to *The Birds of the Western Palearctic*, Vol IV. by S. Cramp, published by Oxford University Press, Oxford (1985).

Biographical Note

Charlie Hamilton James was given his first camera at the age of 13. Since then he has spent over ten years studying and photographing kingfishers on a river near his home in Bristol. He also spends as much time as possible watching and filming otters in Shetland.

Working mainly as a wildlife cameraman and photographer for the BBC Natural History Unit, also based in Bristol, Charlie Hamilton James has filmed kingfishers and otters extensively, as well as travelling further afield to film other animals, such as the rare Ethiopian wolf.